Astr

Michael Beloved

Shiva Art: Sir Paul Castagna

Illustrations: author

Proofreaders: Marcia Beloved / Dear Beloved

Correspondence:

Michael Beloved
18311 NW 8th Street
Pembroke Pines
FL 33029
USA

Paul Castagna
204 Northern Sophie
Bessemer
MI 49911
USA

Email: axisnexus@gmail.com

ISBN: **978-0-9840013-7-8**

LCCN: **2012913750**

Table of Contents

How to use this book:

Make a casual reading page for page without becoming stressed about the concepts and ideas. Read to become familiar with the language style and presentation. If you read something of particular interest make a mental note and read on to get through the entire book.

Make a second reading pausing at areas of interest, where you feel you can grasp the material. Here and there, you may not follow the meanings but read on nevertheless.

Make a third reading with intent to grasp the concepts and suggestions given.

Finally, make an indepth study of this information.

Introduction

This book is long overdue but I did pen some of this information in the Meditation Pictorial book and in many other books which I authored.

In this book however the subject is astral projection and that only. The ins and outs, ups and downs of it, are explained. The layout of the astral world in reference to the physical plane and how one can access it is described.

I made clear in this paper that astral projection is a natural psychic function. It is not something which anyone invented. Nature was doing it since the body was in embryo and continues to perform it every time the physical body sleeps. If any credit is due to the astral projector, it is for being aware of nature's operations.

Astral projection really means becoming aware of one of nature's psychic operations, observing it and figuring how to induce it and use it for psychic exploration. The value of learning astral projection is the familiarity it will give one with the condition one will be in permanently when one loses the physical body.

Everyone without exception will lose the physical body. There is no doubt about that.

What will be next?

To find out:

Become proficient in astral projection.

Dedication:

To Rishi Singh Gherwal, and his disciple Arthur Beverford, who introduced me to asana yoga and brow chakra centering.

And to Amitabha, a Buddha deity in South Korea, who provided much information for this publication

Chapter 1

Astral Projection Defined

Simply put, astral projection is being aware of yourself apart from the physical body. For convention's sake, an individual is his or her material body. When that person discovers itself in a conscious state, making decisions and acting but without respect to the material body, the person is said to be astrally projected away from the physical form.

Astral projection is not the mental act of imagining oneself as being distinct from the body. A person can engage in such imagination. Then it is left to that person to be honest about it. Physically I know if I imagine or if something occurs in the physical reality. I am constantly moving from the real world to the world in my mind, which is a mock-up by the imagination faculty. And yet, I know when something occurs in real terms.

Similarly, when one becomes familiar with the psychic terrain, one distinguishes between real astral substances and mentally created shadow-realities. Some objectivity in psychic states, dreamy occurrences and semi-conscious states are necessary before one can have a clear-cut understanding of the astral body.

If we could get a person's psychic stuffs, his or her psychological content, into one place, that would be the form of the astral body. It is also called a subtle body, an etheric body, a double, a dream body, a body of light, an air body, a mental body, an emotional container.

I was conscious of astral projection experiences when I was less than 6 years of age. At the time I assumed that everyone had such experiences. I never told anyone about it. I thought that it was common for everyone. Later I found out that everyone did not have these experiences. Some people did. Most of them did not understand the experience. These persons tried to rationalize all experiences in a way which supported the conventional opinion which is that each individual is his or her material body

As an infant, I assumed that each person was aware of two bodies; the physical one and the one used in the astral territories. In the culture of my childhood years, people accepted that spirits existed. The idea was that spirits are in the afterlife either with God in heaven, with the devilish beings in hell, or in a state of limbo in an astral world which was directly adjacent to this material place. From that adjacent location, these limbo spirits haunted humanity.

People assumed that there was a subtle body but only after death. During life one did not have that body. During life one only had a material body. Then at death miraculously one assumed a spirit form either as an angel, a devil or ghost. If they stayed in the astral world and did not trouble human beings, such ghosts did not assume a frightening configuration. Instead they lived in the astral dimensions and conducted their lives in those domains.

As a child I saw ghosts who were mostly my departed ancestors. At times, I would feel the touch of a ghost. Then a shrill would ripple through my body. My heart would skip a few beats. My life force would gather its energies as if it was afraid that it would have to leave the body.

I learned early on, not to view dead human bodies. If for one reason or the other, I did, I used to have dreams of horror, where the deceased person would approach me in an astral dimension to demand something or just to spook me.

As a child when there were funerals, most persons would file through the funeral parlor or church to take one last look at the dead body. I would approach the coffin but I would avoid looking at the face of the body. This was an intuitive precaution so as not to meet with the departed spirit as a ghost during sleeping and dreaming.

Persons who are departed become obsessed with the need for contacting their descendants, especially those persons who were very close to them. If they are unable to do so, because the relatives have no psychic sensitivity, they contact anyone else in the vicinity who has psychic perception. They then confront that seer in dreams or even in broad daylight. To avoid being contacted, a psychic should not see the face of a dead body. Visual contact with the features of the dead body of a ghost makes a psychic highly susceptible to the desires of that departed soul. This is why, even as a child, I instinctively did not look at the face of the deceased.

When a body is buried, the relatives may think that the person as its dead body will go into the earth and will be covered over by 6 feet of clay. Actually most persons do stay in the earth for a time with their dead bodies. But even these persons are frequently attracted to and repelled from that dead form. A person who is deceased will try to repossess the physical body, just as they used to when the body was alive. They cannot assume the body as before. They cannot awaken as that form again, but still due to attachment and due to the momentum of their interest in that body, they will make an effort for re-entry. This might go on for days, weeks or months, depending on the person's attachment to the dead body.

The subtle body which a ghost uses is made of radio frequencies. Just as a radio wave might pass through a concrete wall or even enter into the earth, so the subtle body of a ghost can go into the earth and come out of it. This is how a ghost will go into a tomb or go into a buried body and come out of it. This same ghost body can enter into the body of a relative, who might detect its entrance by feeling a shiver, or by feeling cold or by visualizing thoughts from the deceased, or be feeling emotionally-touched by that soul. This can happen.

Consider that the subtle body is called by different names according to the energy level of it. When it is fused into a living physical body, it is called the psyche or the psychological energies of the individual. When it is separated from a living physical body, it is called an astral form. When it is separated from a dead physical body, it is called a ghost or a departed spirit. It is in all cases, the same subtle body in different phases of manifestation.

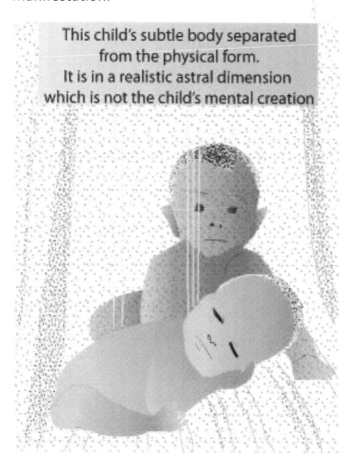

This child's subtle body separated from the physical form.
It is in a realistic astral dimension which is not the child's mental creation

Astral projection is the experience of the subtle body when it is not fused into the physical one. It is a natural experience but it feels unnatural if one is not accustomed to it. It can be an alarming experience. It can be frightening or scary to discover that one can exist outside of the living physical body. Actually at the death of the physical form, that is exactly what happens; one finds oneself as being disembodied, as having lost one's identity and social capacity as the physical form.

I request that you go through this book with an open mind but with the understanding that my experience is just that, one person's credibility. First of all don't be concerned that I am going to change your mind about anything. That is not the plan for this book.

My idea is to reveal that I had certain experiences with an astral body. It does not matter if you had astral experiences. You are not required to accept or to believe my statements. Read this book as you would any book, even as you would a fiction novel.

We see movies of fiction stories or even of true stories which are distorted by movie producers. These do not alarm us because we are not required to believe any of it. And yet even though we are not required to do that, these movies affect us. Something that is plain fiction, that is declared to be an imaginative tale, does not protect us from its influence on our behavior. Something that is unreal can have social impact.

In consideration, I ask readers to go through this book with an open mind. There is no pressure to cause anyone to believe any of this, no more than a fiction writer has that intent. But all the same as fiction affects us this information might affect some readers. I did not write this with malicious intent or with intent to cause anyone to believe or to have faith in me or these experiences. This was written to leave a record of one person's experiences and his resultant convictions. This is intended for information purposes to inform people about the supernatural as it related to being consciously and objectively separated from one's material body while that body lives.

Chapter 2

Increasing Incidences

Persons who had astral projection experiences and who desire to have many more, may be perplexed about a method of increasing the occurrences. A person who has no memory of even one incidence should review the memory to see if there were dream experiences.

Even though many dreams are mental constructions enacted by the imagination faculty of the mind, some dreams are astral projections. I spoke to many persons who say that they cannot differentiate between a dream which is a mental concoction and one which is astral projection.

Some people are doubtful that there can ever be a clear-cut distinction between imagination and astral reality. This is interesting because the same persons claim that they can distinguish between physical reality and imagination of physical reality; perhaps because physical reality appears to be solid, while imagined scenes are the stuff of mental energy. Is everything mental unreal? If you feel that everything mental is illusion, then you will never be convinced about astral reality.

If behind closed eyes a light appears in the mind space, and if after that you deliberately imagine the same light, then the distinguishing factor between the two is the absence or involvement of your deliberation. The mind, however, may imagine a light all by itself without your deliberate visualization. In that case, we have three occurrences:

- The supernatural appearance of a light in the mind space.
- Your creation of a light by exercising your ability to visualize objects mentally
- The mind's independent imagination of a light in the mind space

The second occurrence is done by your deliberate mental action. You use the imagination faculty in the mind to manufacture a light by visualizing that. This is not a naturally occurring light in the astral world. It is a light which was created by your mind. That light will disappear as soon as you do not maintain the visualization of it. This is mental illusion for sure.

The third occurrence is an activity of the mind, which uses its creative energies and produces a light. Your will power is not involved in this. For this you are a mere observer while the imaginative faculties of your mind conduct this construction. This is also a mental illusion.

The first occurrence is the only real experience. This light exists of its own accord in the astral dimensions. You just happen to be on a level of consciousness where you gained access to seeing this astral object.

Astral experiences can be sorted using these guidelines, then the person can know what is real and what is imaginative on the subtle planes. To be able to sort an experience to determine its status as astral reality or imagination, one should practice meditation, while making meticulous observations about the activities in the mind environment.

To increase astral experiences or to initiate them for the first time, you should practice while lying in a comfortable position. If you prefer to sit use a reclined chair, so that your body will be fully supported.

At first make a check to be sure that your body is in a position which is conducive to meditation. You should be rested beforehand. If you attempt this when the physical body needs sleep or when your mind is exhausted, it is likely that you will fall asleep and will not be aware on the astral side.

Are you taking powerful medications, pain killers, prescription or non-prescription narcotics, psycho-active drugs or herbs, stimulants, depressants or any drugs which affect the nervous system of the body? If you are then these procedures may not work to cause conscious astral projection. Are you constipated or taking medications to reduce that condition? Such medications may shut down a part of the nervous system of the body. Which in turn will contribute to a lack of awareness when the subtle body is astrally projected.

Take my word for it, that when the physical system sleeps, the astral form is separated from it.

Astral projection is the condition of being conscious of that subtle body when it is separated. Astral projection is not reliant on anyone's willful action. Nature is already astrally projecting the subtle body whenever the physical one sleeps. Astral projection is one of nature's activities. It is not an activity of identity consciousness in the body. All creatures have subtle forms which separate out of their physical casings during sleep. Becoming conscious of this when it occurs or after it occurred is called astral projection. In a sense the title astral projection is a misnomer because it indicates that this is primarily an activity of the individual concerned. But astral projection is really an involuntary subtle activity of the conjoint subtle and gross bodies which are fused in a life form.

The question is:

Why are most people not aware of this astral projection if it occurs whenever the physical body sleeps?

The answer is hidden in the question itself, because there are so many involuntary activities which are carried out by nature with or without the individual's awareness of it. In fact the body I use stays alive because of the many involuntary acts which occur within it, acts which I am totally unaware of.

Do I digest my meals?

Do I process every bit of thought energy which flashes through my brain?

Do I maintain the billions of cells which are in my body?

Do I manufacture the hormones which are vital to the health of my body?

Did I cause even one hair on my head to grow even one millimeter?

The answer to all of these questions is *No*. And yet these activities take place second after second irrespective of my awareness of them. I can become aware of digestion. I may eat in a way which facilitates that. Similarly I can become aware of astral projection and I can do some things which might cause me to be conscious of segments of that.

To begin the practice of astral projection, accept mentally that the process is already taking place. What you need is to become aware of it. Put your physical body to a resting position when it is not tired and when your mind is not exhausted. Lie comfortably somewhere either in subdued lighting or in darkness. This should be in a place which is adequately ventilated. It could be outdoors provided that your mind remains relaxed and is not disturbed by intense heat or too much cold.

It is recommended that you lay on your side or your back, which ever seems to be the most comfortable. Close your eyes, so that your mind does not wander from object to object visually. Try to relax yourself inside of your head. If thoughts come just let them be. Make no effort to support or banish them. Back away from them by receding into the back part of the head, a place in which thoughts are unable to be formulated. Feel as if you are falling back more and more into the back of the head, away from the noisy thought-filled, image-productive frontal part of the brain.

This is all that you are required to do. The rest is up to nature. If while doing this you fall asleep or doze off, then you are over the first hump in this. There are a few questions to ask yourself about this.

How long this should be done?

Should I set an alarm clock?

If you wish to do this for half hour then you may set your alarm for that period. If you have one hour to spare, then set it for that. As soon as your alarm rings rise and do the needful. Then try again. Try again and again, until something happens and you become aware of yourself as the astral body. It is important that your physical body fall asleep but when you attempt to do this it is also important that mentally you are neither groggy nor sleepy. If you are sleepy it is likely that you will not be aware during the astral projection, and that is the whole aim of the practice.

Some additional ways to increase incidences of astral projection

For those who are aware of the astral body, those who have confidence in the fact that there is a subtle body, you can increase the incidences of astral projection by putting your physical body to rest for a short period on a regular basis, either daily or weekly as the case may be. Be sure that the body is not tired and that your mind is not exhausted.

If the physical body is tired, the life force in the body will require much energy to repair damaged cells in the body. This power consumption will limit the awareness in the astral body when it is separated. In other words, the astral body will separate from the astral one in a sleeping state and will remain asleep during that separation which means that you will not be conscious of it at any stage.

Those who use narcotics and pain killers should realize that these drugs affect the subtle body as well as the physical one. These substances can cause the subtle body to be in a state of stupor or unconsciousness when it is separated. The result of that is astral projection without self consciousness. There will be astral projection in any case, but it will be without objective awareness. In fact the astral body might even be involved in adventures in the astral world but it will do so in a way that is similar to when a person sleepwalks on the physical side. There is activity then but no objective awareness.

Try to do the astral projection session in a location which is different to the area in which you usually sleep. This act of being in another area may cause the mind to regard the session as being special. It might be disinclined from deep sleep in which there is nil self-awareness.

Try to do so on a hard or firm surface. It could be a bed but it should not be a soft bed. In a soft bed the mind might resume its usual sleep activity without self consciousness.

Try to do so when your stomach is not filled. If your stomach is filled and your mind is preoccupied with digestion when you lay down to practice, you may find that you cannot make progress. Besides the mind, the life force in the body which operates digestion and other involuntary functions, will be engaged in digestion.

This might prevent awareness during astral projection.

Cover your eyes. Use a dark cloth over your eyes and forehead to keep light out of the retina and the frontal part of the brain. This might allow your mind to become introverted and to abandon its interest in the external material world.

Keep a dream journal by your bed side and at the place where you meditate. Always attempt to file a report of your mental activities and any psychic experiences which you have. This effort may cause the mind to develop an interest in meditative states and altered states of consciousness which will in the long run, cause you to have increased psychic perception.

Do whatever is necessary to increase astral projection awareness. Observe yourself. Observe when you are astrally aware. If certain circumstances cause an increase in astral consciousness, then note these and incorporate these into your lifestyle.

Chapter 3

You: The Astral Body

I began this life with an "I" which to itself was a material body. It would be wonderful if I was to end this life with an "I" which is the subtle body. This life began with a physical self which considered its psychological energies to be mere accessories. It would be an achievement if in the end of this physical body, that composite of psychic energies had sufficient self-confidence to regard the physical system as its most recent accessory.

Leaving aside the theory of reincarnation, we may begin with the conviction that we are physical bodies. We can then investigate the possibility of transferring our existential confidence from the physical body to the psychological energies. This will not be easy.

How does one even visualize the psychic energies in the form of a body?

What shape would that be?

Would it appear to be similar in formation to the physical system?

Throughout the years, discussing these matters with others, I realized that most persons have little or no confidence in being a subtle body. People cannot get their finger on the trigger of a body which comprises psychological energies. They accept a physical system but cannot envision a psychic personality.

However that is exactly what one should do if one wants to venture into the spiritual side of existence. Look at this partial list of the major components of the human psychology:

- Spontaneous Feelings
- Induced Feelings
- Spontaneous Thinking
- Deliberate Thinking

Look at another list:

- Analyzing
- Conceptualizing
- Emotion transmission
- Emotion reception

This is very simple, isn't it?

What is the shape or form of these psychological energies?

Are these not enclosed in a membrane?

Are these random?

Are these being created and re-created every split second, like the pixels which form an image on a computer screen? Still even in a computer there are certain constant factors. In reference to the images, the screen is permanent.

Is there a permanent backdrop on which the temporary psychological energies function?

Let us consider something else:

In the space where the physical head is located, we experience thought constructions, analysis of ideas, judgment of opinion, mental silence, drowsiness, semi-consciousness, absentmindedness, memory, emotions, interpreted sensual perception and the urge to procure sensual information.

Each of these has its psychological and physical register. The easiest to recognize is the physical process. If I have an urge to acquire something which I see, others cannot verify the urge positively unless I make an attempt to procure the item. Thus the physical counterpart of any activity has become the conventional method of certifying it.

To develop psychic perception one has to leave aside this physical verification method. Even though the physical method can be evidenced by multiple witnesses, it still does not help us with the psychic registry. To develop psychic perception, we have to increase confidence in subjective perception. This means that we cannot expect to get verification from others. In fact sharing experiences with others may result in the curtailment of inner psychic research. Most persons will speak in a discouraging way about non-physical verification.

If the psychological energy were to take shape what would that be?

My proposal is that it would be a mirror image of the physical system. A ghost is only a mirror image of a physical body. It is made of subtle energy.

Can I become used to the subtle energy, to the psychic stuff. I accept it in electronics. It provides communication services through cell phones, videos and numerous digital devices.

A phone message which is a subtle energy signal, is not always coherent. In some phone calls, the sounds come in broken pieces with some missing to such an extent that we cannot tell what was recorded. And yet we have confidence in the electronic mechanisms.

Why not extend the same leeway to psychic perception?

To consider the self as a subtle body, as a composite of psychological energies, we need only imitate what we are already doing with the physical body. The physical body is a composite of material substances. By convention, we accept that as the self. This acceptance process or identity application may be shifted to the subtle aspects of the physical system.

During a dream can I consider the dream body to be my real self?

Why not?

It is no more speculative than considering the physical body to be the person, something which I did by convention from the time I became conscious as this body.

Should I first determine if I am the body?

Should I dissect that to see if that is a false identification?

Not necessarily.

So far it served the purpose to be the physical body. Why complain about that now. I can switch to being the subtle body. I can view myself as composite psychological energies in the form of a subtle body, a person of psychic stuffs instead of a person of material solids, liquids and gases combined into one body.

Chapter 4

Zones of the Astral World

Ideas of a real astral existence are surmised from dream experiences which are basically of three types. These are:

- Exalted convincing spiritual experiences
- Mediocre dream experiences which are quite similar to earthly life
- Demeaning and horrible experiences which are similar to a hellish earthly life

Conventionally speaking these are described as being heavenly, earthly or hellish conditions. In fundamentalist religions, the afterlife is considered to be either a hellish or heavenly one, based on faith of the deceased at the time of death. For the purpose of this discussion I want to regard the astral world as having three areas. First there is the earth-similarity area, which is a place which is adjacent to this physical world.

It is the place where most human beings find themselves aware during astral projections. This place is a purgatory holding area for spirits who must take another material body. These persons will again become physical infants. For one reason or the other, they cannot get a body immediately and so they remain in the earth-similarity area for days, weeks, months or years. Then they again come out in the physical world as babies of women.

The second astral zone is the lower astral planes, where one may become horrified by hell beings, devils, mischievous entities and persons who have a deteriorating astral disease. These are considered to be lower astral planes because the energy in these locations is dense and heavy. A person who was mostly criminal during the earthly life, or one who had a terminal disease, or one who was politically vicious, might go to a lower astral plane after death. After staying there for some time, the person's flaw diminishes. The subtle body changes in constitution. Then the person automatically transits to the earth-similarity area to wait for a new physical body.

The third astral zone is the heavenly world. Some persons who have near-death-experiences (NDE) described their transit to such places. People who are religious are usually hopeful of attaining these places after death. They feel eligible because of religious affiliation.

In my experience with heaven, it is usually attained in a flash and it disappears from view very quickly. I am convinced that attaining such places after death is possible for only for a split second or more. Immediately after, the person would find himself or herself in astral places which are similar to life on earth. He or she will wait there until taking birth as a baby on this or a similar planet.

The question is: If we accept the premise that everyone has a subtle body which is a composite of their psychological energies, then how does a person qualify for life in the higher astral world, the heavens, the paradises, the residences of benevolent deities?

Is it a matter of faith as some religions advocate?

Is it based on a person's social behavior?

Will a person, who is prone to criminal acts, transit to a hellish astral place on the basis of the energies in his subtle body.

Will a person who is not very good and not very bad, just go to an earth-similar astral place after death, merely because he or she was not especially criminal and was not exceptionally saintly?

In this physical reality, we see that a politician, who was prone to propaganda, may develop throat cancer. Sometimes a police officer, who kicked many prisoners, comes down with leg paralysis. Sometimes a woman who serviced prostitution gets a fatal uterine infection.

Is this evidence that human behavior is causal?

How about the exceptions where the man who shot many persons criminally, died peacefully in a luxury villa? It is obvious that he who exploits violently may not die in a bloody way. Can we be sure? Suppose nature reacts proportionally but delays some responses?

My proposal is that a person should implement a life style which is consistent with what that persons wishes to be in the afterlife. What have I to lose if I do that? If there is no afterlife, then I would have fulfilled myself to the best of my ability during this short contribution which I made to the earth's history. If on the other hand there is an afterlife, then I will gravitate to a place which is compatible to what I desire.

If you want heavenly life after death, live in a way which is similar during life. For instance do you want to live under conditions in heaven where you have to keep and then kill animals for food?

In the afterlife, would you like to live in a place where there are criminally-minded persons?

Who do you encounter in dreams?

Do you meet hell beings, mediocre people or lofty beings of a saintly and divine nature?

So much of what we are and what we do hinges on the social environment. Assume that it is the same with the astral zones. If you were to record your dream experiences and subtle impressions upon rising from sleep daily, what percentage of those experiences would be hellish?

How much would be heavenly and divine?

How much would be similar to events in the physical world?

Chapter 5

Escape from the Lower and Adjacent Astral Places

Once you enter an undesirable astral place, you may have to remain there under the force which attracted your subtle body. Trying to escape is not the solution. It is best to observe what happens there, note the influences, participate and then slip away when you can but with the information regarding not what happened but what forces compelled your subtle body to go there.

After returning to the physical side from an unfavorable projection, you should carefully go over every detail of the experience, with a keen eye as to the force or forces, person or persons which caused you to be there.

It is not where you go but who or what was the force-energy which compelled the astral body to transit there. Will power is a side feature in the astral world. Freedom has little meaning there. In the astral domains it is all about influence. Once an influence expresses itself in the astral world, one may have to submit until it expires. The real issue is not what happened but who or what caused it.

Lower astral planes

One is pulled into a lower astral plane because of one of three reasons:

- Criminal activities
- A link with someone who is on the lower astral level
- Missionary work for a divine being

Of the three reasons, the only one which concerns the person who is pulled is his or her criminal or socially-detrimental acts. These are acts which are already committed; hence their effects cannot be reversed. Once an act is committed, its reaction is in the works and will arrive in the fate of the doer either today, tomorrow or in the far flung future. The doer cannot avoid the reaction if he or she remains in a zone where that reaction would manifest. If there is no escape, the only sensible way out is to face the music and let the reaction take its course.

One should not be like a bear which when caught in a steel trap fatally tears its limbs apart. That will cause more injury than the escape is worth. One should have confidence that the incidence will soon subside. One will be released. No one stays in hell forever. All hell beings are released sooner or later since their duration in hell is based on their offenses against nature. No one has eternally been offending nature. Everything has duration in these realms. Hence a hell being can only remain for as long as the effect energies of his nature-disapproved acts are not exhausted.

Those who transit to astral hells on the basis of previous association with persons, whose criminal acts cause them to be there, will be released from the place as soon as they deposit a certain energy to the party concerned. A simple example from everyday life could illustrate this.

A man performed some services for which he was not paid. The person who received the services found that at the termination of the work, he could not pay the worker. That employer agreed to pay the worker as soon as he would have the funds.

In the meantime, that worker was arrested for a theft which he committed. The judge decreed that he should pay a fine or be imprisoned for six months. The accused told the judge that an employer owed him an amount which was half the fine. The judge said that if that money was paid to the Clerk of Court, then the accused would serve half the time, three months and then be released.

After being sent to the prison, the accused send a message to the employer asking for the wages. At first the employer disregarded the notice. He felt that since the man was in prison, nothing could be done about it.

However the prisoner filed a formal complaint at the court. Subsequently the employer was served a notice to either pay the said money or appear before a magistrate. To avoid having to deal with the legal authorities, the employer paid the wages.

This caused the prisoner to be released after 3 months, which was half the jail term.

In this incidence, we see that the employer was circumstantially forced to go to a hellish place which is the prison. Once there he only stayed as long as it took the wardens to take the prisoner's wages and write a receipt. The employer had to go to the hellish place but only for a short duration. Similar the prisoner also stayed there for a short time. In fact his six month sentence was cut in half because of the service to the employer previously.

No limited entity can situate itself in such a position to have an eternal criminal record. Thus no entity will remain under hellish conditions forever. One should be confident that one will be released from a hellish astral place as soon as the effect energies which caused one to be there, are exhausted.

There are incidences where one is transited to a hellish place by a divine being. The reasons for such transit vary but it usually has to do with being selected to be a teacher and a person of divine influence to persons who are criminally entrapped. Persons who develop criminal habits and who cannot seem to break the pattern, are sometimes selected for special assistance. A divine being will then instruct a saintly person to assist such persons who are in hellish conditions in the astral world and who have so much of a criminal record, as to be worthy of a long time in the astral horrors.

Any person, who serves a divinity in this way, will be taken out of the hellish environment as soon as they perform the missionary service which was assigned.

The lower astral realms are sometimes called the nether regions or the subterranean places. These are not gross environments but when one's astral body transits to these places, the locations seem to be gross. This is because the subtle body's energy level is synchronized with the frequencies of such places during the transit. In certain dimensions, light is solid to light, water is solid to water and air is solid to air. In some experiences, the astral projector may enter kingdoms which are within the subtle body of the earth. These places are astral realities.

Adjacent Astral Realms

There are places which are adjacent to the earth but which are in other dimensions which are very close to the vibration of the physical substances on earth. These are parallel worlds. When one transits to any of these places, one notices the similarity between these places and the earth. Usually these locations are such that there is not much technological progress. These places act as a relief valve, a stress-free existence, for those departed souls who were neither worthy of an astral heavenly place nor condemned to an astral hell.

When one goes there one may find that the people are friendly. They offer hospitality and employment. Such a place is the likely destination of most human beings after death of the physical body. In dreams, people in an adjacent parallel world may try to induce one into staying in those territories but if one's life on earth is not exhausted, one cannot stay in those astral places.

Those invitations serve to alert the person that after death of the physical body, one will assume full identity as the subtle form and will again meet such persons. One may assume permanent residence in one of those places. To avoid that fate, one should investigate the reason for the attraction, then endeavor to remove it. If it is based on a relationship with a deceased relative or friend, one may seek to transit to another astral level which is out of reach of that other person. If one fails to do so, one will, more than likely, go to that place after death of the physical form. One will then stay there for a time, after which one will come out again as a baby of woman on the physical side, and with no memory of the former life.

Chapter 6

Perspectives: Astral Body

The astral body is a real form but it is made of mental and emotional energy. This is why it is illusive. This is why some persons disbelieve it. By convention, we render the most confidence to what is physical, what is solid and what can be apprehended by the physical body.

The astral body rapidly changes in vibration and that makes it even more difficult to pin-point. The physical body remains in one vibrational plane for its life duration but the contents of the astral body may decrease or increase in frequency. This makes it difficult to detect and categorize.

The confusion about the existence of the astral form is compounded further because we have an imagination faculty which can compose ideas, images, and other media perceptions. To distinguish between an actual psychic perception and an imagination is not easy.

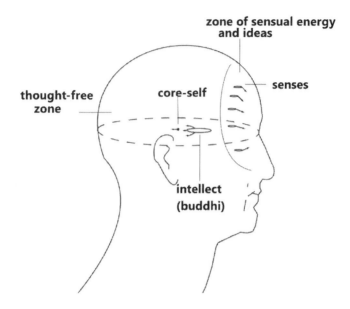

By repeated practice at astral projection and at studying the schematic of consciousness in the silence of the mind, one might develop the ability to reduce imaginative operations. If one reduces the imaginations, one's ability to sort actual psychic activity would proportionately increase. There was a great yogi-philosopher in India whose name was Patanjali. He recommended the reduction and eventual illumination of the imaginative operations of the mind. His advice is very beneficial for those of us who want accurate psychic perception.

Belief is both the friend and the enemy of mankind. After realizing its disadvantages, many people pretend that they are free of it but actually we cannot be free of belief entirely. In all circumstances we must use faith. For instance, even to breathe one must have confidence that there will be air available. That is subtle but it is a system of belief. For understanding the subtle body one should be open to the ideas of it as described by persons who profess it.

We can be certain that some persons will tell untruths but that should not prevent us from having an open mind. The risk is there that someone will exploit or con others but that is a risk which we take everywhere in any contact with others. One's mind may also mislead one from time to time.

When one has an astral experience, it may be very clear. It may not be abstract and confusing. This means that one will become aware of an astral projection objectively. As I stated before astral projection is taking place whenever the body sleeps. If there is no memory of it, the person is in an unconscious or semiconscious state which does not support observation or recall of the experience. Astral projection really means that nature allows one to be objectively aware while the subtle body is separated from the physical one.

To facilitate observation and recall of the experience, I recommend lying down on a hard surface or reclining and doing so when one is fully rested. One should set a time such as 20, 30, 40, or even 60 minutes so that after that time one can rise and continue with daily routine.

DEFAULT POSITION OF CENTRAL CONSCIOUSNESS

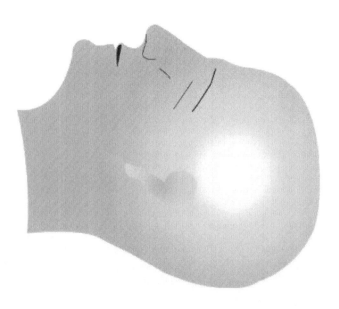

CENTRAL CONSCIOUSNESS VICTIMIZED BY THOUGHTS

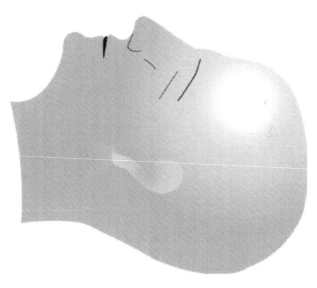

CENTRAL CONSCIOUSNESS NOT VICTIMIZED BY THOUGHTS

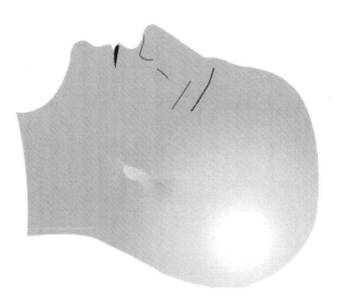

If there is no experience, one should not be discouraged. Just try on the following day. Be patient. When you lie down or recline to do this, leave aside cares and concerns, just feel as if you are falling to the back of the head away from the frontal part of the brain where various images and ideas abound.

I was conscious of astral projection since infancy. I was lucky. But that does not mean that you cannot have these experiences. Again I remind you that astral projection is not your deliberate action. It was not mine. It is not something that I commanded myself to do. It happened. Astral projection is happening but you have to achieve consciousness of its occurrence.

Beware of pain killers and other drugs which affect the life force of the body. Any drugs which affect the nervous system might deter objective awareness of astral projection. If someone says that he or she does not have dreams, the real meaning is that this person is not aware during dream experiences. Dreams are taking place regardless of whether the person is aware or not.

Dreams can be astrally projected activities. They could be psychic activities when the astral body is not projected. Or they could be imaginations.

I gave three types of dream occurrences. Let us see this in a listed format:

- Astrally projected activities
- Psychic activities which take place when the astral body is still fused with the physical one
- Imaginations which take place while the physical body sleeps

Some dreams are only imagination. These are mental and emotional constructions in the mind which is the head space of the subtle body. These are psychic actions which take place within the mind of the individual.

Other dreams are psychic actions which take place while the subtle body is interspaced in the physical, when the subtle body is not separated from the physical one. These are real psychic actions even though they take place while the two bodies are still fused together. Unlike imaginative dreams, these occurrences take place in a real astral environment which is outside of the mind of the dreamer. Imaginative dreams are different. They occur in the internal environment within the mind of the dreamer. These other dreams occur outside the mind of the dreamer but in a psychic dimension.

The other type of dreams is psychic actions which the subtle body commits when it is separated out of the physical form. This occurs in a real subtle world and may not affect what happens on the physical side of existence. In this situation the dreamer is the subtle body. One acts with that body in an external psychic environment. One can also think in the head of that subtle form, just as one would think in the brain in the physical form while one is in the physical environment.

If you have dream experiences learn how to sort them. If you have no dream experience, then if you are taking any type of prescription or non-prescription drug, make an effort to cease taking these. Of course if there is a life and death matter, then you may have to remain taking these just for the sake of keeping your body alive, in which case, you may have this information even though you are unable to apply it.

Drugs which dull consciousness and affect the nervous system to decrease pain for instance, will not be available after the body dies. Hence if you have this information now, it might be of use to you when you leave the body. Then you will be left with your mental and emotional energy as yourself with no material body to contain it.

I do not run a church or a religion. I am not involved in a business enterprise. For that matter money is the least of my concerns. I realize that I will soon have to abandon this body. What is the use of conning people and amassing money if I will have to leave it all behind. I feel responsible to provide this information. That is why I wrote this book.

You are not required to believe or accept what I stated. The main thing is that this information should stir you to investigate your psychological survival after death of the physical you. If there is any chance that all or part of the emotional and mental part of you will survive, then this information is of value.

Chapter 7

Distinction:

Dream/Astral Projection

Many people who have direct experience of astral projection fail to accomplish it because their belief structure stipulates that astral projection is mental fantasy. To these folks, any object which is not physical has to be an imagined substance which exists merely on the strength of the imaginative powers of the mind.

Any experience which occurs in a drowsy or sleeping condition may be termed as a dream but one should not dismiss every such experience as being reliant upon and created by the imagination faculty. As I define it, a dream is really an astral projection in which the dreamer has little objectivity. In such a dream the dreamer's imagination faculty is certainly at work. But it operates also in the person's waking condition. We do not object to its operation when the person is externally aware, so why criticize it only when it functions in dreams. The problem is the lack of discrimination during dreams.

To give the mind a sense of accountability of what happens when the physical body sleeps, one may keep a dream journal by the bedside.

One should develop a habit of noting what happened in dreams as well as whatever came to mind when one arose from sleep. This simple action will increase the likelihood that one will be more objective in dream states. This will increase the degree of clarity during dream experiences.

How does a person know when he visualizes himself throwing a ball and when he actually does so?

The same discrimination applies in dream states.

The key factor is the location of the incidence. Was the dream only in the mind, which is in the head of the subtle body? Was the dream outside of the mind, outside of the head of the subtle body but inside of the psychic environment which is exterior to the subtle form?

Did the dreamer experience another-ness within his mind, such that he felt that someone entered his mind environment, entered the conventional "me".

If someone enters the mind environment which is the head of the subtle body, that invader is an alien to that environment. The dreamer's interactions with the alien are real psychic events.

In the mind environment, there can be imagined events which are merely mental and emotional constructions but there can also be real psychic events such as the entry of other persons and the dreamer's interactions with them.

The man entered a car which entered a garage which was located in a house which was located in a city on an earth, which is in a solar system, which is part of a galaxy which is part of the universe.

Compare the car to the psyche! Within the car, the man can do many things. He can speak to himself. He can activate its radio. He can start the engine. This is like the dreamer doing things in his own mind. But suppose a friend of the driver is allowed to sit in the car. The driver can converse with his friend in the vehicle. In addition, he can wind down the window, and give a donation to a beggar. That beggar is an object which is outside the car but which is in the environment in which the vehicle travels.

The dreamer can meet people within his mind space and also outside of it. In both cases, the dreamer and the other person are individual realities, irrespective of each other.

To realize if I am imagining or actually seeing a physical object, I need to distinguish if the object relies on my imagination faculty or if it has independent register. During dream experiences, one can maintain clarity if one's imagination faculty stops its automatic creative mode. For persons whose imagination is always operating, they should curtail that creativity. Then they would have clarity about imagined instances as dreams and real psychic interaction as astral behavior.

Both in waking consciousness and dream states, there is interaction between imagination and reality. In waking states, however, one is more likely to accurately distinguish between the two. The difficulty with the dream states is obvious but that does not mean that everything in dreams should be relegated as fantasy or imagination.

A physical object is so far from an imagined idea of the same, that it is easy to distinguish between two, mostly because of the grossness of physical reality, and the subtleness of mental creations. Since imagined dreams are made of the same material as psychic reality, distinguishing between the two is not as obvious. One requires psychic sensitivity if one is to have clarity in the matter.

A person with a very sensitive mind, who is detached from his or her imaginative operations, can know if a subtle experience is a mental concoction or a real instance of psychic actions. That person can also sort a mixture of imagined events in dreams which takes place at the same time as actual psychic occurrences.

But what of others?

Can anyone else develop that sensitivity?

Chapter 8

Practicing Astral Travel

The most important way to begin the astral travel practice is to first give credit where it is due, which is to nature and not the person who is sponsored by nature. I am the person who exploits nature but I am not the cause of astral projection. The separation of the subtle body from the physical one, occurs by a process of nature which is activated successfully every time the body sleeps. It is that last sleep of the body which is marked as death, where the astral body will be unsuccessful in reconnecting into the physical form. But even death is a nature-process even though the individual can have some minor adjustment either in postponing it or accelerating its occurrence.

We move in this world by the grace of nature. We took these bodies and actually became aware of ourselves as these bodies at birth, all by the actions of nature. The individual spirit is necessary in these operations but its necessity is as a power source, a focal point, not as a designer. The system is designed by nature while it uses the spirit's energies in its operations.

The methods in this book have to do with admitting first of all that nature operates astral projections successfully without the conscious assistance of the person who uses the astral and physical bodies.

Can you deal with this information?

Does this information discourage you?

Are you thinking that this cannot be true?

I discussed methods of increasing the incidences of astral projection. I return to that subject again:

- Lie or recline on a firm surface which is not your usual resting place.
- Do so when you are thoroughly rested.
- Set a time limit for this practice. It should be between 20 minutes to 60 minutes.
- Cover your eyes and forehead with a dark cloth.
- If possible be in a room which is in darkness or in subdued lighting. Alternately you may

practice when the sun is overhead or at sunset with your body in alignment with the sun so that your forehead catches the rays of the sun in a centralized way.

- Mentally sink back into the back part of the head, retreating from the frontal part of the brain which is the area in which thoughts and images flash impulsively.

DEFAULT POSITION OF CENTRAL CONSCIOUSNESS
MIND IN NEUTRAL STATE WITHOUT THOUGHTS

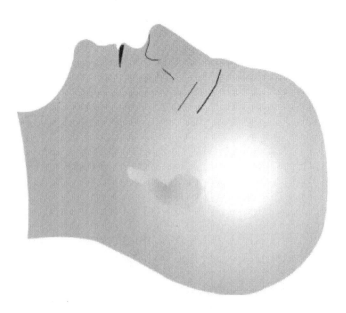

CENTRAL CONSCIOUSNESS VICTIMIZED BY THOUGHTS

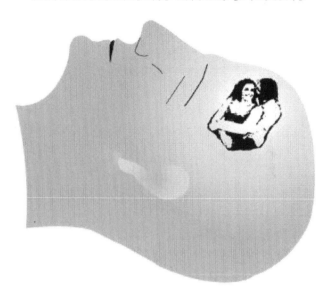

CENTRAL CONSCIOUSNESS NOT VICTIMIZED BY THOUGHTS
BECAUSE OF ABANDONING THE FOREBRAIN AREA

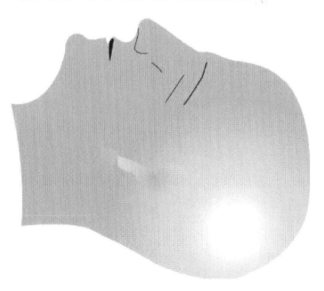

- You may imagine yourself floating above the physical body. Or you may imagine that your psychological energies have the form of the physical body and are detached spatially from the physical system. This imagination is imagination only. It is not astral projection. It is not an actual mystic act. However in some people, this visualization leads to actual separation of the astral body. Just as a man who thinks of drinking liquor and visualizing himself doing so, may soon after actually go to a bar to purchase a drink, some persons were successful at projection by imagining the separation and then experiencing it as a psychic fact.

- Imagine that you have a body which is made of water vapor, of the same type of energy as a cloud. Imagine that this body floats out of the physical one and rises to the level of the clouds. This is imagination to be sure and is not an actual projection but it might lead to conscious subtle body separation.

- If you hear a sound in the head, a high pitched frequency sound, try to connect yourself into it, to fuse yourself in it. Trace its source and go into that.
- If you see a light in the forehead area or if you see a cloud of energy or vortex of energy or a disc of energy which is stationary or moving, then focus on that psychic object. This may lead to astral projection.

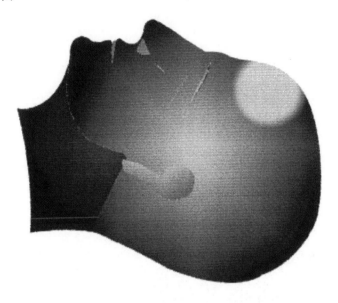

Set aside a time to practice. This could be a daily or weekly assignment. Be sure that you select a time when your body and mind are rested and free of stress. Use an alarm clock if you have one. Limit the time for practice between 20 and 60 minutes. Lie down or recline on a firm surface. If possible this should not be the bed where you sleep. Choose a different area.

The mind associates a certain bed with sleeping; hence it may go into sleep mode if you attempt to practice there. If possible do this practice anywhere besides the bed or matting where you usually sleep.

As soon as you lie down or recline, cover your forehead and eyes to prohibit light from entering your brain in that area. This is necessary to cause the mind to renounce its interest in the physical forms. The eyes are used by the mind to pursue colors and forms. If the eyes are open or if light makes contact with the eyes, the mind may try to pursuit objects in the external environment. This will cause the mind to increase its thought operations. This is not conducive to conscious astral projection.

After securing a blindfold where the forehead and eyes are covered to keep out light, you should check your mind's content.

What thoughts, images and ideas are present?

Can these be ignored?

If you can ignore these, then the mind will be silent because it cannot operate thoughts, images and ideas without getting attention from the core-self, the observational identity region of the mind. A silent mind is a boon for increasing the likelihood of conscious projection.

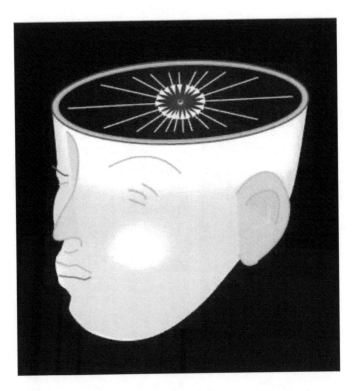

If the mind has many thoughts or images or if the mind has only a few of these, you should try to retreat to the back of the head. In the back region, thoughts and images do not arise. On the psychic plane, the impressions arise in the fontal part of the brain. If you retreat backwards, the impressions will stop or be reduced considerably.

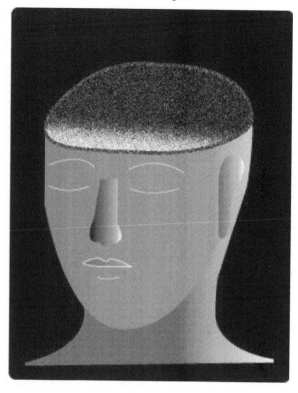

When there is a relative sense of calm in the mind space, you should make a decision either to wait for an astral projection to occur or to do things which might induce nature to cause a transit. Remember that astral projection is an operation of nature. You might be able to induce nature to separate the astral body if you remain silent in the mind or if even you were to begin visualizing your subtle body as being distinct from the physical one.

This visualization is not astral projection. You should not indulge yourself in the fantasy that it is. It is not but still visualization may be instrumental in causing a projection. After visualizing yourself as a psychic being rising away from your subtle body, you should relax, stop the visualization and just wait in silence to see if nature will separate the two bodies, allowing you to consciously observe the process.

When as a child, I used to astral project, it would be mostly when I took day naps. At the time I did not know that most human beings were not having these experiences or were relegating them to being just dreams and fantasy. Later when my body was about 20 years of age, I began to rest with the intent of becoming conscious when the subtle body was separated.

I knew it was nature's operation. I never thought of it as something I regulated. I knew the thing for me was to be conscious when nature projected the subtle body. If I fell asleep and then woke without being objectively aware during the sleeping process, I knew that like a sleep walker I was either unaware of my astral activities or I had the experiences but could not recall them.

Instead of working to control astral projection. I endeavored to be aware of it when it occurred. I used to lie on my back with my palms upwards or with palms down and fingers touching over my torso. I would pull my chin up and back. Then I would focus either on the back of my head or between the eyebrows.

Sometimes after 15 or 20 minutes, something would happen. It might be a loud thunder clap. It might be a flash of light. Something would happen on the psychic level. Then I would realize myself as being the subtle body distinct from the physical form.

There were many reports of persons who separated out of the physical body and who said that they looked and saw the physical form lying on a bed sleeping or being handled by surgeons. For me this occurred very infrequently.

Usually when I would astral projection, I would not see the physical world. I would only see the subtle environment to which my subtle body had transited. When I saw physically, it would be when my astral form had synchronized into the physical one and I was enabled with physical perception again. In some rare circumstances, there would be no vision at all. It would be like my subtle body had no eyes or like its eyelids were sealed. I would move about in the total darkness of my mind space on these occasions. I was in an astral environment but I was like a blind person moving in a space which he could not visually perceive.

I have astrally projected into locations where I could see the environments. If people were there, only some of them would see me. In several of these experiences, I would rise into the air as my subtle body would float. Then some persons who were there and who were unable to float would reach up to pull me down. These persons would be perplexed about levitation. I would mentally cause the astral body to raise high enough to be out of their reach.

Rarely was I attacked by someone else when I astral projected. This is because I usually found my astral body in an astral world where the people were benevolent and desirous of being with me. When I was attacked which was infrequently, I would either try to defend myself or move out of reach of the attacker. This always resulted in my astral body being pulled back into the physical one. I would wake up as the physical body with the memory of those undesirable astral events.

In one or two experiences, I woke up and then went back to sleep immediately, seconds after, and found myself back in that undesirable astral place. I would then flash back into my physical body and wake it up. I would try to stay awake and not to sleep immediately after. I felt that my astral body would return to the same place if I did.

There was a time when I was in Denver. This was around 1973. I used to lie outdoors on a lawn at noon when the sun was overhead. I used to put a dark cloth over my eyes. The sun would be positioned centrally over my forehead. I would invariably astral project like this day after day for months.

In these experiences, my third eye would open just before I astral projected. These projections were vivid and clear. Once when I astral projected my astral body made a rapid transit to the sun planet. Then after I spoke to some persons there, it returned. This happened in 30 minutes during a lunch break.

During those years, my conclusion was that astral projection is best practiced during the day, when the body is not sleepy, on a firm surface and not on the bed where one sleeps.

There is one specific experience which I should describe here. Sometime in 1973, I was travelling alone in a Volkswagen car from Denver, Colorado to Kansas City, Missouri. The highway was long and boring because this is a relatively flat land once one gets away from Denver.

Somehow I began to nod out even though I had sufficient sleep. Then I nodded out and lost control of the vehicle. There was a deep graded slide to the right of the highway. The car went into the air and somersaulted.

As it was doing that I became fully conscious in my astral body which had instantly separated out of the physical form. Then I found myself in that astral body which was made out of light and I was looking down at the crumpled up physical form. In those days, seat belts were not mandatory, so the physical form had moved and when the car landed up-sided down in the ditch by the side of the road, it was crumpled up like a large sleeping bag which was folded in a sloppy way.

I looked at the body with interest and not even recognizing that it was my body. I was so detached from the whole experience that it was like looking at something which happened to someone else.

Then suddenly I was drawn into the physical body and I then came to my senses about what happened. In a way I appreciated the incidence because of this most valuable firsthand experience of the fusion and separation of the astral form from the physical one.

When I fused back into the physical body it was not harmed even though it was folded over. I got out of the vehicle, rolled it over and as soon as I attempted to drive away I was flagged by a highway patrolman who promptly wrote a reckless driving ticket. He began to measure the skid marks of the vehicle and drew his own conclusions.

In this experience, when the astral body separated, it had no sense of the condition of the physical form and when people depart from a body, they do not carry with them the pains and aches of the dying physical form unless the subtle body itself has those health problems.

Chapter 9

Sensational Events
before Astral Projection

An astral projection has a specific initial point which is rarely witnessed even by the best of the mystics. This is because material nature hides the process of how it unifies and separates the physical and astral forms.

Unless one meditated for some time, and became renounced from social involvements, it is hardly likely that one will experience the separation and subsequent unification of the two bodies. More than likely, one will fall asleep before an astral projection, become aware that it happened, and then find oneself awake in the physical form with memory of the experience. The separation and the reunification processes will hardly be observed.

When I was isolated for a time, away from social involvements, practicing meditation regularly, I was empowered to observe the separation and unification processes.

After lying down or reclining, I might hear a loud thunder clap which would be an internal, mentally-heard sound only. There might be flashes of lightning in the mind space or down in the body. The area of the third eye might have an oval or circular shaped cloud of energy moving towards or away from me, through the forehead. In some experiences just before the two bodies separate, there may be a tunnel of light which was widest near to me and which narrowed the more distant it was from me. The tunnel may be whirling.

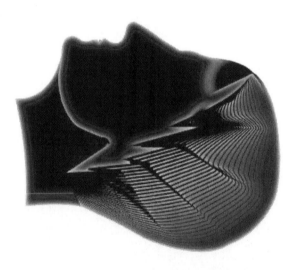

In other separations there was the sound of rushing winds like a terrible storm or tornado.

Sometimes there was a vacuum draw which seemed to be extracting the subtle body from the physical one.

Then suddenly the two bodies would be separate. I would no longer be aware of the physical one. I would only be aware of the astral form. The same awareness which I had of the physical one would now be as the subtle one. Just as one feels identical with the physical system when it is awake, that is how it is with the subtle one during a projection, except that the subtle body might be floating.

In some experiences it would be floating at a certain speed of its own accord and I would not be able to stop it or slow it down. In other experiences I could control its flotation. Then I could move faster or slower as I willed.

The astral environments are different to the physical one but some looked physical, having qualities which seem just as if it was the same earthly place. Sometimes I would float into a wall and being fearful of crashing into it, I would try to stop the subtle body from approaching it. If perchance it did not respond to my will power it floated through the wall. I never had an experience where the subtle body could not pass through a material but the fear that it might not was present on many occasions.

The decision to return to the physical body, to wake up on this side of existence as the usual physical body-self hardly arises during astral projection. This is because the experience is just as valid as life on the physical side. Hardly anyone who uses a physical body thinks of an alternate existence or of transferring to another dimension. Usually with a dead-ended consciousness people are preoccupied with social concerns here.

In an astral projection one becomes involved in the particular dimension one finds oneself to be in. One participates there just as one does in the earth's history. However if during an astral experience an anxiety arises in the mind, as for instance where I felt that I needed to get to the place of employment or that I should meet a commitment at a certain time, one will find that one is immediately yanked back into the physical body and will get up as the physical body with or without memory of the astral event.

It does occur that in sudden awakenings, one becomes conscious of the physical side and then after some moments, one finds oneself back again outside of the physical body in another dimension as the subtle form.

Psychic Life-force System

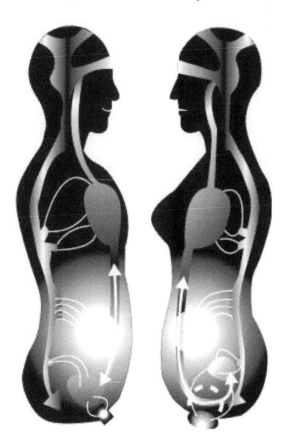

There is a mechanism which controls the astral body. That is called the life force or kundalini. The name kundalini was assigned by yogis in India. It indicates a coil compressed psychic force which directs life activity. The easiest way to understand this force is to study the involuntary functions of the body, particularly those which transpire from moment to moment and which we are hardly aware of. These include digesting, excreting, inhaling, exhaling, heart pumping, cell manufacture, cell repair, sleeping, waking and numerous other involuntary reflexes and functions. The life force conducts these motions with or without the assistance of the person involved.

This life force causes the separation of the astral and physical systems. It then causes the reunification of these bodies in a synchronous way. If this life force fails to cause a complete synchronization of the two systems, one experiences sleep paralysis (cataleptic trance) or death. Coma is another word for sleep paralysis except that coma is prolonged sleep paralysis. When the bodies are in the process of separating or being unified, sleep paralysis can occur.

Involuntary functions are conducted by one psychic mechanism which is the kundalini life force. When the kundalini psychic conductor is unable to do its functions, we have problems with the material body. To get some insight into this kundalini we may study sexual expression. The energy for sexual intercourse is accumulated by and expressed by the kundalini.

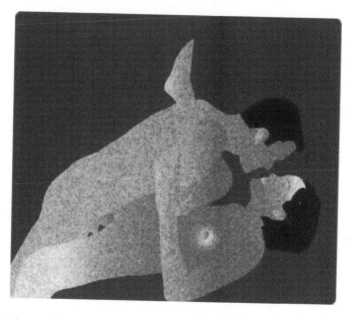

The internal flashes, sounds, and other sensational psychic occurrences which mystics and psychics describe in reference to astral projection, are conducted by the kundalini life force, not by the person who is projected. Observation of the activities of this life force gives insight into how the two bodies merge and are distinguished when they are separated.

Mismanagement of the kundalini life force causes coma, epilepsy and related incapacities. The individual self is there but it is serviced by the kundalini and cannot function properly as a physical body or as an astral form, if the kundalini is not perfectly executing its functions.

There are adjacent parallel worlds which are very close in frequency to the physical situation. Usually one is drawn into such worlds during dreams. One's subtle body is drawn there by one's ancestors and by dearly departed friends. In these places, there are roads and buildings such that the subtle body seems to be physical when it is in those domains. There it does not float but stays put on land and sinks into water but does not drown if it does so.

Persons who are departed and who have not gone to higher astral worlds, heavens, and who have also not gone to subterranean astral places, hellish domains, usually stay in the adjacent astral world, for months or years until somehow they are attracted to parents on this side of existence. Once attracted, they enter the emotions of those people and if by a miracle they come out as babies in this world.

Persons who live in those astral domains find that their consciousness still remains referenced to the lifestyle they had on earth. Thus they exert influences which cause the subtle bodies of their descendants to be drawn into those domains during the sleeping periods on earth.

When one discovers oneself to be there during a sleeping session, one may not even realize that the place is an astral domain. One might perform in it as one would in any dream. However specific features of these experiences single them out as more than imaginative scenes.

After these sojourns, one feels compelled to think of the person or persons one met in the encounter. There is a give and take in the mind with one speaking to the person and the person replying, which is actually a session of telepathic thought exchange.

Chapter 10

Final Astral Projection
Death

Astral projection is a nature-function but it will run its course when finally the material body is no longer fit to be a biological unit. At that time when the vital functions cease, the physical body will deteriorate because the psychic life force which monitored its life will itself be vacated from the physical system.

At the time there will be one last astral projection and the person involved may or may not be aware that this final exit of the subtle body has occurred. Yet, even for those of us who will not know when death of the physical body has occurred, even they will know of it as soon as they become objectively aware as astral forms.

After death, some of us will feel ourselves existing and not see the astral form which we exist as. Otherwise one will feel and also see the astral form just as a person with physical vision can perceive the outside of his or her material body.

Psychics usually make that final transit in full or partial consciousness. A psychic may be aware of the final exit and the permanent transplant of the life force from the physical system into the astral system only. But such a life force is usually carrying with it a tendency to hastily acquire another physical body.

Advanced yogis, highly evolved entities and divine beings carry in the subtle body a no-need for physical form. This frees them from the urge for looking for new parents as soon as the physical body is no longer part of the psychology.

A person who has some psychic perception can maneuver during the death experience, can stage part of it so that it is not shocking and so that there is a sense of purpose as to what to achieve when the physical body is taken out of conscious range of that individual.

The process is to transfer the psychological tendencies from the physical system into the astral body as the death experience transpires. These psychological components will go with the self regardless but if the person can expedite it, then in the afterlife there will be memory of the life experiences and the person can use those conclusions to chart a better course in the next material body if there is to be one.

For those who will not take another material body, the transfer is done leaving certain aspects behind. These unwanted features are not transferred from the physical system to the astral body and instead these remain in the lower astral dimensions where they are promptly confiscated by other entities on the astral plane who feel they could use the discarded energy.

After leaving a material body for good, a spirit is left to consider the purpose of that previous earthly life.

What should a spirit do after it discovers itself thinking and psychically acting but having no access to being part of the physical history of the earth?

What should it do after the religious hopes fizz out?

After there is no salvation, no kingdom of God, no non-existence, only existence as a sense of feeling to exist, then what?

When the atheist passes on and finds itself in the astral world for good, thinking, having seen or not having seen a divine being, then what should that person do next?

When reaching out to relatives who still have material bodies, if one finds that they have no psychic perception, then what?

When looking back and remembering how one lived on earth, the control one had, the participation in history which one was allowed, then how should one conduct thoughts and feelings in the astral domain?

When realizing that despite the death of what one was, which is a material body, still one continues to exist like will-'o-wisp or a flimsy thought , then what?

When after discovering that one is no longer alive, that one is surely dead, and when seeing ghastly beings who threaten to inflict one with punishments, then who will one rely on?

When understanding the stark truth that death is absence from physical history but presence in some flimsy astral dimension, then how will one reconcile the layout of the hereafter in reference to the physical reality which one knew but no longer can utilize?

The final separation means that there will be no more wake-ups to claim a certain social identity. This is bewildering even to the most stalwart philosophers and even to mediocre yogis who knew that it would happen anyway.

Am I ready for it today?

Do I want to postpone it for as long as possible even to the extent of thinking that maybe I will be the exception and it won't happen?

Who will take my property?

Will it be used in my interest?

How can I exert some influence over how my assets will be used?

Should I leave it all behind and focus on the shifty astral dimensions, develop a lifestyle there and renounce everything that I worked for in my past life?

What would happen in the astral existence once it becomes my permanent habitat and I no longer can awaken on the physical side? Will I find a dimension which is like a paradise, a place where everything desirable is available?

What would that paradise be like?

Could I reside there forever or will it be a fleeting experience like the flavor of ice-cream?

Will I find a sexual companion there?

Will babies be taking birth there?

Will those who were there for the longest period be facing terminal diseases, infirmity, dementia and death?

How does an astral body deteriorate?

How does it feel?

Are there astral hospitals?

Is there an astral prison world?

What happens to those human beings who performed criminal acts in their last bodies?

Do they have to face ghost police at the time of final departure from the body?

Are there governments in the astral domains?

Is there a God or gods who preside over the dimensions?

What is right there?

What is wrong?

Are there people whom I may exploit there?

Is there a measure of human intelligence?

Can I be competitive there, outclassing others and taking advantage of their stupidity?

Can I be an astral being for all the future?

Chapter 11

Final Astral Isolation

Physical Life Begins

Once a person dies to this physical world, being cast away from its history as it were, then the astral existence begins with no respite to escape into physical existence as that person once did after the physical body slept and then rose for social conduct in the earth's history.

Death of the physical body is another way of saying that a person is sentenced to a fulltime life of astral projection. That person, who used to escape from nightly dreams and dimensional encounters by waking up in this world as a social somebody, is now without access to physical existence, barred for the time being from making a direct mark on history.

Some powerful mystics wield power from the astral world by influencing others who have material bodies. The mystic inspires embodied persons to work physically to fulfill desires and to spread particular teachings on the physical side of existence.

They achieve this by attracting the astral bodies of embodied persons to their astral presence and then exerting varying degrees of influence. In this way long after leaving a physical body, they continue to focus their interest into the gross material world.

For the ordinary person, death of the physical system is no boon. It is regarded as a great loss of opportunity. Such people long for a chance to again be an integral part of the earth's history. Even those who have no idea about the recurrence of life which is reincarnation, hope to again reenter into history. They would give anything for a chance to be a physical somebody.

The astral isolation does not last forever for anyone who desires physical life and who misses opportunity in creature existence. Sooner or later, all depending on the energy in the psyche, such persons again get another body.

What happens is that their astral existence reached a dead-end, where their hopes for physical life max out, their attachments for physical people draw them to a birth location, a place where two humans or even two animals are engaged in sexual intercourse. There they feel that there is a standstill for them. Their consciousness becomes frozen as if astral time stood still. They enter a trance-like state, forget everything about themselves and everything else, remain still for some months and wake up again as an infant of a female somewhere somehow in the world of physical bodies.

Then as they loop back into the gross existence, they begin a new round of unconscious astral projections, until at last again the physical system dies and they are again set loose in the astral dimensions to again feel dissatisfaction for not being part of the earth's history.

This is the cyclic story of existence.

Chapter 12

Translation – Astral Body Ends

The basic layout of existence is this physical world in which we are currently centered and focused; then there are the dream dimensions, the astral world. These two existences are the way of existence for most human beings. But there is yet another existence which transcends even the astral world. That is the spiritual world.

In ordinary religion the astral world is the spiritual world, where the lower astral regions are the hellish situation, the median ones are adjacent to the physical existence, and the higher ones are the heavenly worlds of the deities.

The spiritual world is beyond the higher astral regions and the view of it is not possible except by special dispensation from a divine being.

Even the higher astral world is off limits and cannot be accessed except by the grace of deities who regulate entry into such places.

But who bars one from entry?

No one bars anyone. That is not necessary. The restriction for access is by the vibrational content of the subtle body. Souls with a lower vibrational content have no access to higher systems and do not even conceive of such places. They utterly disbelieve in the existence of the heavens.

Those who accept that such a place may exist but who are vibrationally antagonistic to those paradises, are barred from actual experience of those locales by the content energy of their subtle bodies.

The divine world is fabulous beyond a person's wildest dream. No one can go there who would be incompatible with the Supreme Person. No disharmony with the Supreme Being can exist there. Everyone and everything there is in constant loving attraction to the Supreme Entity.

The astral heavens give one a hint of that spiritual place which is beyond everything on this side of existence. Very few spirits become translated there.

Encouragement
Astral Tours

It is a good idea to tour the astral domains. Getting a preview of the world I will be in, once my physical body dies, gives me insight into the transit my subtle body must take in the near future. What is it, seventy or one hundred and one years for the most, and then I must leave the physical form?

Anyone who must migrate would do well to be briefed on the outcome before he leaves his native land. What will I look like in the astral world?

What will I wear?

Who will be my mother or father?

What is the environment?

Is it cold? Is it hot?

How will I be treated?

What will be my status?

Will I have to be educated?

Will I have a sex urge?

Will I marry to someone?

Will I have children?

What job will I take?

Is it scenic or drab?

Will my subtle body die in the future?

Who rules in the subtle world?

Are there prime ministers?

Are there armies and commanders?

Is there a God?

Are there gods?

These questions and more are of interest in the subject of the subtle body and the hereafter. Astral projection can solve some of the riddle of whether there will be an afterlife, and as to the conditions of such existence.

The observational perspective is what is needed to come to grips with the astral body. The separation of it from the physical which is a well-kept secret of nature, can be observed if the dreamer is in an observational position in reference to his own subtle form or that of others.

By meditating in silence regularly, one can develop the sensitivity required to observe astral projections. But even if one cannot do that, one can at least realize an astral projection while one is aware in the course of it. The man in the train may not remember how he stepped into the train. He may not remember how he stepped off the train when disembarking. He may recall scenes which flashed by as he stared out of the window during transit.

What will I wear?

There is no crisis for garments in the astral world. There, a person wears whatever is mentally desired. If for instance a young lady desires a different color hair, she can produce that effect merely by thinking of it. But this is only true in certain astral worlds, on certain levels. In other astral places, a person cannot change appearance merely by will power.

The lower astral world is rife with paradox and limitation, while the higher astral dimensions are the places with varying degrees of legendary freedoms. Generally in the astral world one takes an appearance that suits one's intentions and demeanor but there are lower astral places in which good people appear to be villains and vice versa.

What to do?

My suggestion is that you should think of attire as being formed on the basis of the person's character. The more honest and sincere one is, the less conniving and the less untrustworthy, the more likelihood there is that one will have a desirable appearance.

Angelic women in the astral world assume whatever form and color they desire. They are as pretty as they deem themselves to be. They can change their forms and even adapt as forms of other women secretly. I have had many experiences in the astral world where an angelic woman who is not my spouse on earth, assumes the form of my spouse, approaches me and relates to me just as my spouse would. This does happen in the astral world. If however you are an honest and sincere person, you will realize that the person has done this but you may not figure that during the experience. You may realize it soon after the occurrence.

There is an illustration of this in the story of King Pururavas. He fell in love with an angelic woman named Urvashee. They got married but unfortunately for the King, Urvashee left the earth and went back to the heavenly kingdom. Later she came to the earth while there was a religious festival in India. When the King saw her, he went out of his mind over her. She agreed to stay for a short time. After sexual intercourse, Urvashee left for the heavenly world. Then again a year after the King saw her on earth again. He pleased her and she agreed to stay with him again but she substituted one of her servants for making love with him.

This servant assumed the form, complexion and mannerisms of Urvashee. Initially the king did not know that his angelic wife substituted this woman. Later when he analyzed everything he realized that he was tricked.

As for what to wear and how to appear with what features, with what complexion or race, one should not consider this: Rely on your character to form a suitable subtle body in the hereafter.

Who will be my mother or father?

There is a nice indication from Jesus Christ about parenting in the heavenly planets. When he was asked about the selection of a husband in the hereafter by a woman who while on earth had more than one sexual partner, Jesus replied that in the kingdom of heaven, there is no marriage or official assignments of spouses to anyone.

This does not mean that there are no situations of sexual mates. In the heavenly world, those who are sexually attracted to each other stay together by the force of that attraction. Living together is not a formal institution which is licensed by the church or state.

In some heavenly worlds, one angelic male might have several angelic females as partners or one angelic female may have several angelic males at her beck and call. No one takes birth as a baby in the astral worlds. If a woman desires a child and if she is in a permissible astral dimension, a child will appear as her infant. In most of the angelic worlds, the concept of having children through sexual intercourse and childbirth does not occur. It crosses no one's mind. It is not an idea which occurs in those environments.

However, in the astral world there are maternal, paternal and fraternal relationships. These surface automatically but without a sexual family basis as their cause. These are spontaneous situations which arise due to the soul to soul connections.

If a human being is very attached to someone else, that human being will leave the body and go to the hereafter with the sentiment. It will then seek the person to whom it is attached. If the person assumed another material form, it may take another body to be with that person.

Attachment is a strong force in the astral world. The control of it is the key to being able to select the astral region one prefers. In all cases, in the tossup between attachment and preference, attachment will dictate the circumstances on the astral planes. Attachment is the most powerful force in the astral world. It supersedes every other type of preference.

Definitions

Astral projection is being aware of yourself apart from the physical body.

Astral projection is the condition of being conscious of the subtle body when it is separated from the living physical form.

When the astral body is fused into a living physical body, it is called the **psyche** or the **psychological energies** of the individual

When the **psychology** of the individual is separated from a living physical body, it is called an **astral form**. When it is separated from a dead physical body, it is called a **ghost** or a **departed spirit**. It is in all cases, the same subtle body in different phases of manifestation.

The last astral projection of the subtle body is marked as **death** of the physical form.

Death is absence from physical history but presence in a flimsy astral dimension.

Index

Author

Michael Beloved (Yogi *Madhvacarya)* took his current body in 1951 in Guyana. During infancy and childhood he had many conscious astral projections as well as sleep paralysis bouts which lasted for the most about 2 minutes. He assumed that this was a natural state and that each person overcomes this in the process of time just as infants have an imbalance when learning to walk but master it nevertheless even if they lack confidence. During the early teen years, Michael tried to study sleep paralysis on his own without mentioning anything to senior relatives. In 1965, while living in Trinidad, he instinctively began doing yoga postures and tried to make sense of the supernatural side of life.

Later in 1970, in the Philippines, he approached a Martial Arts Master named Mr. Arthur Beverford. He explained to the teacher that he was seeking a yoga instructor. Mr. Beverford identified himself as an advanced disciple of Rishi Singh Gherwal, an ashtanga yoga master.

Beverford taught the traditional Ashtanga Yoga with stress on postures, attentive breathing and brow chakra centering meditation. In 1972, Michael entered the Denver Colorado Ashram of *kundalini* yoga Master Harbhajan Singh. There he took instruction in bhastrika pranayama and its application to yoga postures. He was supervised mostly by Yogi Bhajan's disciple named Prem Kaur.

After learning kundalini yoga, Michael realized that astral projection was caused by the kundalini life force's action of displacing the astral form from

the sleeping physical one. He investigated the cause
of this and discovered that if the kundalini was kept
in a super charged state one would be conscious of
the astral state.

Series

Commentaries

Yoga Sutras of Patanjali

Meditation Expertise

Krishna Cosmic Body

Bhagavad Gita Explained

Anu Gita Explained

Kriya Yoga Bhagavad Gita

Brahma Yoga Bhagavad Gita

Uddhava Gita Explained

Yoga Sutras of Patanjali is the globally acclaimed text book of yoga. This has detailed expositions of yoga techniques. Many kriya techniques are vividly described in the commentary.

Meditation Expertise is an analysis and application of the Yoga Sutras. This book is loaded with illustrations and has detailed explanations of secretive advanced meditation techniques which are called kriyas in the Sanskrit language.

Krishna Cosmic Body is a narrative commentary on the Markandeya Samasya portion of the Aranyaka Parva of the Mahabharata. This is the detailed description of the dissolution of the world, as experienced by the great yogin Markandeya who transcended the cosmic deity, Brahma, and reached Brahma's source who is a divine infant Krishna.

Bhagavad Gita Explained shows what was said in
the Gita without religious overtones and sectarian
biases.

Anu Gita Explained is the detailed description of
the effect-energy of current actions in application
to future lives.

Kriya Yoga Bhagavad Gita shows the instructions for those who are doing kriya yoga.

Brahma Yoga Bhagavad Gita shows the instructions for those who are doing brahma yoga.

Uddhava Gita Explained shows the instructions to Uddhava which are more advanced than the ones given to Arjuna.

Bhagavad Gita is an instruction for applying the expertise of yoga in the cultural field. This is why the process taught to Arjuna is called karma yoga which means karma + yoga or cultural activities done with a yogic demeanor.

Uddhava Gita is an instruction for apply the expertise of yoga to attaining spiritual status. This is why it is explains jnana yoga and bhakti yoga in detail. Jnana yoga is using mystic skill for knowing the spiritual part of existence. Bhakti yoga is for developing affectionate relationships with divine beings.

Karma yoga is for negotiating the social concerns in the material world and therefore it is inferior to bhakti yoga which concerns negotiating the social concerns in the spiritual world.

This world has a social environment and the spiritual world has one too.

Right now Uddhava Gita is the most advanced informative spiritual book on the planet. There is nothing anywhere which is superior to it or which goes into so much detail as it. It verified that historically Krishna is the most advanced human being to ever have left literary instructions on this planet. Even Patanjali Yoga Sutras which I translated and gave an application for in my book, **Meditation Expertise**, does not go as far as the Uddhava Gita.

Some of the information of these two books is identical but while the Yoga Sutras are concerned with the personal spiritual emancipation (kaivalyam) of the individual spirits, the Uddhava Gita explains that and also explains the situations in the spiritual universes.

Bhagavad Gita is from the *Mahabharata* which is the history of the Pandavas. Arjuna, the student of the Gita, is one of the Pandavas brothers. He was in a social hassle and did not know how to apply yoga expertise to solve it. Krishna gave him a crash-course on the battlefield about that.

Uddhava Gita is from the *Srimad Bhagavatam (Bhagavata Purana),* which is a history of the incarnations of Krishna. Uddhava was a relative of Krishna. He was concerned about the situation of the deaths of many of his relatives but Krishna diverted Uddhava's attention to the practice of yoga for the purpose of successfully migrating to the spiritual environment.

Explained Series

<u>**Bhagavad Gita Explained**</u>

<u>**Anu Gita Explained**</u>

<u>**Uddhava Gita Explained**</u>

The speciality of these books is that they are free of missionary intentions, cult tactics and philosophical distortion. Instead of using these books to add credence to a philosophy, meditation process, belief or plea for followers, I spread the information out so that a reader can look through this literature and freely take or leave anything as desired.

When Krishna stressed himself as God, I stated that. When Krishna laid no claims for supremacy, I showed that. The reader is left to form an independent opinion about the validity of the information and the credibility of Krishna.

There is a difference in the discourse with Arjuna in the Bhagavad Gita and the one with Uddhava in the Uddhava Gita. In fact these two books may appear to contradict each other. In the Bhagavad Gita, Krishna pressured Arjuna to complete social duties. In the Uddhava Gita, Krishna insisted that Uddhava should abandon the same.

The Anu Gita is completely different to the Bhagavad Gita. Krishna refused to display the Universal Form. He quoted a siddha from a higher dimension who lectured on the effect-energies of actions as these construct a person's future opportunities.

Meditation Series

Meditation Pictorial

Meditation Expertise

The speciality of these books is the mind diagrams which profusely illustrate what is written. This shows exactly what one has to do mentally to develop and then sustain a meditation practice.

In the **Meditation Pictorial**, one is shown how to develop psychic insight, a feature without which meditation is imagination and visualization, without any mystic experience per se.

In the **Meditation Expertise**, one is shown how to coral one's practice to bring it in line with the classic syllabus of yoga which Patanjali lays out as the ashtanga yoga 8-staged practice.

Both books are profusely illustrated with mind diagrams showing the components of psychic consciousness and the inner design of the subtle body.

Specialty Topics

sex you!

The mystery of sex and reincarnation is explained in detail, not in terms of religion or superstition but by psychic facts which any individual can observe, if he or she can shift focus to the psychic plane. Books like the Bardo Thodol (Tibetan Book of the Dead) and the Egyptian Book of the Dead (Papyrus of Ani), along with Bhagavad Gita, the reincarnation teaching of Buddha and other vital books, took humanity through a spiritual technological leap through time into the hereafter. Perhaps none of these texts dealt with the incidences of sex and reincarnation head on, especially the link between you and the sexual act of your parents which produced your body. In this book you get the details in plain terms without mystery and religious impositions.

Spiritual Master

Practically every positive and negative aspect of having a guru is discussed in this book with recommendations of how to deal with gurus safely. A non-proficient guru can be useful despite his faults, but one must know how to side-step hassles and get to the business at hand, which is to get effective techniques from a spiritual master.

In some cases the spiritual master will be a complete fraud but one should not let that deter one from making spiritual progress in his association. "But why," one might ask, "should one stay with a fraudulent guru?" The answer is that if providence puts one in that position, one should honor providence but one should do so without getting hurt by the unqualified spiritual master. This and similar topics are discussed in this book.

Sleep Paralysis

A short to-the-point paper on the psychic cause of sleep paralysis, how to manage it and decrease incidences.

The relationship between sleep paralysis and astral projection is explained. The methods of decreasing the incidences of sleep paralysis, increasing dream recall and being objectively conscious during astral projections is described.

The most revealing part of this paper is the author's description of his sleep paralysis states and what he did to contain these, get out of these and cause his psychic self to separated from and to fuse into the physical body without an incidence.

English Series

Bhagavad Gita English

Anu Gita English

Markandeya Samasya English

Yoga Sutras English

Uddhava Gita English

Uddhava Gītā English

Michael Beloved / Madhvacharya das

These are in 21st Century English, very precise and exacting. Many Sanskrit words which were considered untranslatable into a Western language are rendered in precise, expressive and modern English, due to the English language becoming the world's universal means of concept conveyance.

Three of these books are instructions from Krishna. **In Bhagavad Gita English** and **Anu Gita English**, the instructions were for Arjuna. In the **Uddhava Gita English,** it was for Uddhava. Bhagavad Gita and Anu Gita are extracted from the Mahabharata. Uddhava Gita was extracted from the 11th Canto of the Srimad Bhagavatam (Bhagavata Purana). One of these books, the **Markandeya Samasya English** is about Krishna, as described by Yogi Markandeya, who survived the cosmic collapse and reached a divine child in whose transcendental body, the collapsed world was existing. Another of these books, the **Yoga Sutras English,** is the detailed syllabus about yoga practice.

My suggestion is that you read Bhagavad Gita English, the Anu Gita English, the Markandeya Samasya English, the Yoga Sutras English and lastly the Uddhava Gita English, which is much more complicated and detailed.

For each of these books we have at least one commentary, which is published separately. Thus your particular interest can be researched further in the commentaries.

The smallest of these commentaries and perhaps the simplest is the one for the Anu Gita. We published its commentary as the Anu Gita Explained. The Bhagavad Gita explanations were published in three distinct targeted commentaries. The first is Bhagavad Gita Explained, which sheds lights on how people in the time of Krishna and Arjuna regarded the information and applied it. Bhagavad Gita is an exposition of the application of yoga practice to cultural activities, which is known in the Sanskrit language as karma yoga.

Interestingly, Bhagavad Gita was spoken on a battlefield just before one of the greatest battles in the ancient world. A warrior, Arjuna, lost his wits and had no idea that he could apply his training in yoga to political dealings. Krishna, his charioteer, lectured on the spur of the moment to give Arjuna the skill of using yoga proficiency in cultural dealings including how to deal with corrupt officials on a battlefield.

The second commentary is the <u>Kriya Yoga Bhagavad Gita</u>. This clears the air about Krishna's information on the science of kriya yoga, showing that its techniques are clearly described free of charge to anyone who takes the time to read Bhagavad Gita. Kriya yoga concerns the battlefield which is the psyche of the living being. The internal war and the mental and emotional forces which are hostile to self realization are dealt with in the kriya yoga practice.

The third commentary is the <u>Brahma Yoga Bhagavad Gita</u>. This shows what Krishna had to say outright and what he hinted about which concerns the brahma yoga practice, a mystic process for those who mastered kriya yoga.

There is one commentary for the **Markandeya Samasya English**. The title of that publication is <u>Krishna Cosmic Body</u>.

There are two commentaries to the Yoga Sutras. One is the **Yoga Sutras of Patanjali** and the other is the **Meditation Expertise**. These give detailed explanations of the process of Yoga.

For the Uddhava Gita, we published the **Uddhava Gita Explained**. This is a large book and requires concentration and study for integration of the information. Of the books which deal with transcendental topics, my opinion is that the discourse between Krishna and Uddhava has the complete information about the realities in existence. This book is the one which removes massive existential ignorance.

Website:

https://sites.google.com/site/michaelbeloved/

Forum:

http://meditationtime.grou.ps/

Contact:

axisnexus@gmail.com